Audit Report

OIG-SBLF-11-001

SMALL BUSINESS LENDING FUND: Investment Decision Process for the Small Business Lending Fund

May 13, 2011

Office of Inspector General

Department of the Treasury

Contents

Audit Report 1

Results in Brief 2

Small Business Lending Fund 4
    Program Status 6
        Investment Decision Process 9

The Program Targets Institutions with Adequate Capital for Lending and Repayment,
but Small Business Lending Potential Will Not Be Fully Assessed 14
    Capitally-Impaired Banks are Ineligible for the Program 14
        Potential for Growth in Small Business Lending Will Not Be Fully Assessed 15

SBA Lending History Will Not Be Considered 17

Other Opportunities for Improvement 17

Recommendations 20

Matter for Congressional Consideration 25

Appendices

    Appendix 1:   Objectives, Scope, and Methodology 26
    Appendix 2:   Comparison of TARP – CPP/CDCI and SBLF 28
    Appendix 3:   Management's Response 33
    Appendix 4:   Report Distribution 34

Abbreviations

CDCI	Community Development Capital Initiative
CDFI	Community Development Financial Institution
CDLF	Community Development Loan Fund
CPP	Capital Purchase Program
FBA	Federal Banking Agency
FDIC	Federal Deposit Insurance Corporation
FRB	Federal Reserve Board
OIG	Treasury Office of Inspector General
SBA	Small Business Administration
SBLF	Small Business Lending Fund
TARP	Troubled Asset Relief Program

OIG

The Department of the Treasury
Office of Inspector General

Audit Report

May 13, 2011

Don Graves, Jr.
Deputy Assistant Secretary for Small Business, Housing, and Community Development

This report presents the results of our audit of the investment decision process for the Small Business Lending Fund (SBLF) and provides an overview of the program's status. SBLF is a $30 billion fund that was created to provide capital to community banks with assets of less than $10 billion with incentives to stimulate small business lending. Our audit objectives were to determine whether: **(1) the decision process established by Treasury ensures that eligible institutions in need of capital or with the most potential for small business lending are approved, and (2) investments are made in institutions with good track records for performance and compliance with small business lending requirements.**

At the time of the audit, Treasury had established an investment decision framework, but major elements of the framework had not been finalized, providing the Department of Treasury Office of Inspector General (OIG) an opportunity to recommend improvements early in the development stage. Therefore, our audit focused largely on the first two stages of the process that were most defined—the initial eligibility check and Federal Banking Agency (FBA)[1] consultation, which were finalized in March 2011. We reviewed pre-decisional policies and procedures for other stages of the investment decision process, but sufficient information was not available to perform a detailed analysis.

To accomplish our objectives, we reviewed the concept of operations for the decision process, procedural guidance, memoranda of understanding (MOUs) between Treasury and the FBAs, consultative decision templates to be used by the FBAs and evaluation checklists established by Treasury.

---

[1] The FBAs are the Office of the Comptroller of the Currency, the Office of Thrift Supervision, the Federal Deposit Insurance Corporation (FDIC), and the Federal Reserve Board (FRB).

We also reviewed the program application form, outreach guidance to eligible institutions, and program terms. We interviewed SBLF program staff, contractor personnel, and officials from each of the FBAs. The interviews with the FBAs involved discussions about their processes for determining the financial viability of institutions applying for capital under SBLF. In addition, we met with officials from the Small Business Administration (SBA) to discuss potential lender performance and compliance data as well as small business lending market statistics that could be shared with Treasury officials. We conducted our fieldwork from January through March 2011 in accordance with *Government Auditing Standards*. Appendix 1 contains a more detailed description of our objectives, scope, and methodology.

Results in Brief

Treasury launched the SBLF program on December 20, 2010, but has not issued the program terms for all applicants. Currently, only insured depository institutions, bank holding companies, and savings and loan holding companies may apply for funding under the program. As of April 18, 2011, Treasury had received 626 applications from these institutions requesting approximately $9.2 billion. Approximately 43 percent of the applications were from Troubled Asset Relief Program (TARP)[2] banks. Treasury officials estimate program terms will be released for S corporations, mutual institutions, and Community Development Loan Funds (CDLF) in May. Although it is too early to tell how many institutions will ultimately apply to the SBLF program, Treasury expects that less than two-thirds of the $30 billion will be requested.

As of April 8, 2011, Treasury has also not finalized its investment decision process for evaluating SBLF applications. Treasury submitted applications to the FBAs for review as early as January 2011, but it did not finalize the terms of the FBA reviews until March 15, 2011. Although many areas of the process are still incomplete, Treasury expects to fund the first institutions in the second quarter of calendar year 2011.

Our review disclosed that Treasury's investment decision process, which closely follows legislative requirements, targets institutions that are at least adequately-capitalized because the Small Business Jobs Act of

---

[2] The TARP program consisted of several initiatives, which included the Capital Purchase Program (CPP) and the Community Development Capital Initiative (CDCI).

2010[3] restricts participation to financially viable banks. Financially viable banks are adequately capitalized, not expected to become undercapitalized and not expected to be placed into conservatorship or receivership. According to Treasury officials, this requirement will increase the likelihood that participants, including banks currently participating in TARP capital programs, can repay their investment and have sufficient capital with which to increase small business lending. However, TARP banks approved for SBLF funding are not expected to get much additional capital beyond their outstanding TARP investment balances. The maximum investment for TARP banks, like other institutions, is restricted to a percentage of their risk- weighted assets, and for many TARP banks, such assets may have declined due to the downturn in the economy since the time of their application to TARP.

To a lesser degree the process focuses on the applicants' ability to achieve their small business lending goals. Applicants are required to submit small business lending plans that include their small business lending goals, but neither the FBAs nor Treasury intend to review the plans for the likelihood of goal achievement. Treasury program officials also do not have a formal plan to consult with SBA or leverage market data that SBA may collect to determine the attainability of goals reported even though the Small Business Jobs Act provides that Treasury may consult with SBA regarding the administration of the SBLF program. SBA officials stated that they welcome consultation with Treasury as it would provide an opportunity to: (1) help Treasury maximize SBLF program outcomes; and (2) put institutions in touch with SBA resources for developing outreach plans and business strategies to target small businesses in the areas they serve. Finally, Treasury does not plan to consider the small business lending history of applicants who are SBA lenders to identify institutions with compliance issues. Senior Treasury officials indicated they are interested in having the SBLF program office explore ways to leverage SBA's data and experience to achieve program outcomes.

Our audit also identified other areas where the investment decision process could be strengthened. Specifically, we determined that: (1) although FBAs are required to disclose only material supervisory issues, they have significant discretion on which issues to disclose to Treasury;

---

[3] The Small Business Jobs Act of 2010, Public Law 111-240, was signed into law on September 27, 2010.

(2) Treasury has provided no specific guidance to the FBAs for identifying banks that may be required to raise matching funds; (3) the noncumulative treatment of SBLF dividends, which are driven by capital requirements imposed by an amendment to the Dodd-Frank Wall Street Reform and Consumer Protection Act of 2010 (Dodd-Frank Act)[4], may result in institutions not fully paying all of the expected dividends for Treasury's investment; and (4) the financial performance of applicants may change between the time of the FBA review and the disbursement of funds, creating a need to update supervisory information provided by the FBAs.

We are recommending that Treasury report to Congress monthly aggregate data regarding the capital ratios of applicants approved for SBLF funding, which is publicly available in call reports. We are also recommending that Treasury evaluate the reasonableness of small business lending plan goals before making investment decisions and consult with SBA in making the evaluation. Treasury should also discuss with SBA compliance issues associated with SBLF applicants who are SBA lenders; confirm with FBAs that there are no changes in an institution's financial viability or new supervisory concerns prior to disbursement of SBLF funds; and develop matching capital guidance for the FBAs detailing Treasury's expectations.

In addition, we are suggesting that Congress consider whether a legislative amendment to the Small Business Jobs Act or a waiver from provisions of the Dodd-Frank Act is needed, to make the repayment of all dividends a requirement for exiting the program.

Small Business Lending Fund

Program Eligibility

The SBLF is a $30 billion fund created by the Small Business Jobs Act to stimulate small business lending by providing capital to community banks with under $10 billion in assets. Banks with total assets of $1 billion or less may receive capital investments equaling up to 5 percent of their risk-weighted assets. Banks with total assets of more than $1 billion may receive investments of up to 3 percent of their risk-weighted assets. The SBLF also provides an option for eligible banks to refinance preferred

---

[4] The Dodd-Frank Wall Street Reform and Consumer Protection Act of 2010, Public Law 111-203, was signed into law on July 21, 2010.

stock previously issued to Treasury under two TARP initiatives—the CPP and the CDCI programs. To be eligible for refinancing, an institution must be in material compliance with its CPP or CDCI agreement, be current on its dividend payments to Treasury, and have not previously missed more than one dividend payment. In addition, all outstanding CPP and CDCI securities must be refinanced, with SBLF funds, or repaid in full at the time of the SBLF investment. If approved for less SBLF funding than their outstanding TARP investments, institutions must also pay the difference, ensuring that the TARP investments are repaid in full.

An institution is not eligible for the SBLF program if it is on the FDIC's problem bank list or has been removed from the list in the previous 90 days. Generally, this will include any bank with a composite CAMELS[5] rating of 4 or 5. Treasury may also require some institutions to raise matching funds as a condition for program approval. Banks seeking refinancing of their CPP or CDCI securities cannot be considered for approval on a matching funds basis.

An institution interested in applying for funding must submit an application to Treasury and a small business lending plan to its FBA, which includes the institution's lending goals, the basis for the goals, and how it intends to use the funds to increase small business lending.

SBLF Investment

Treasury will provide participating institutions with capital by purchasing Tier 1 qualifying preferred stock or equivalents in each institution. The price an institution pays for SBLF funding will be reduced as the bank's qualified small business lending increases. The increases in small business lending are measured against a baseline of outstanding loans in the four quarters ending June 30, 2010. As defined by the Small Business Jobs Act, qualified small business lending comprises loans of up to $10 million

---

[5] The CAMELS rating system is an international bank rating system through which bank supervisory authorities rate institutions from 1 (best) to 5 (worst) on six components: capital adequacy, asset quality, management, earnings, liquidity, and sensitivity to market risk. Each component rating is weighted and an overall composite rating of 1 to 5 is assigned to each bank. A composite CAMELS rating of 1 is the highest rating and represents the least supervisory concern, indicating the strongest performance and risk management practices relative to the institution's size, complexity, and risk profile. A composite CAMELS rating of 5 is the lowest rating and represents the greatest supervisory concern, indicating the most critically deficient level of performance and inadequate risk management practices relative to the institution's size, complexity, and risk profile.

to businesses with under $50 million in annual revenue within the following categories:

- Commercial and industrial loans;
- Owner-occupied nonfarm, nonresidential real estate loans;
- Loans to finance agricultural production and other loans to farmers; and
- Loans secured by farmland.

The cost of capital provided through SBLF would start at no higher than 5 percent, and could fall to as low as 1 percent depending on the institution's increase in small business lending. For every 2.5 percent increase in the institution's qualified small business lending, the initial 5 percent dividend rate would drop by 1 percent. The dividend rate would be adjusted quarterly for approximately the first 2 years (9 calendar quarters), and then be locked in for the next 2.5 years. Rate reductions would apply only to the portion of the SBLF investment that is equal to the dollar amount of the increase in small business lending. For example, if an institution received an SBLF investment of $5 million and increased its qualified small business lending by $4 million, the reduced dividend rate is applied only to the $4 million.

If an institution does not increase its small business lending in the first 2 years, the cost of SBLF capital rises to 7 percent. If a CPP or CDCI institution refinances under SBLF, but fails to increase small business lending after approximately the first 2 years (10 calendar quarters), the cost of capital will increase by an additional 2 percent annually for the next 2.5 years. After 4.5 years, the dividend rate for all SBLF participants becomes 9 percent.

Program Status

Treasury officially launched the SBLF program on December 20, 2010, approximately 3 months after the Small Business Jobs Act was signed. Although the application process was opened to most institutions in December 2010, Treasury has received only 626 applications, requesting approximately $9.2 billion as of April 18, 2011. Although it is too early to tell how many institutions will ultimately participate in the SBLF program, it is unlikely that all of the $30 billion authorized for the program will be requested if the current rate of applications submitted continues.

Treasury currently expects to distribute only one-half to two-thirds of the $30 billion authorized for the program.

Of the total applications received, 271, or 43 percent, were from institutions currently participating in TARP CPP and CDCI programs. The amount requested by TARP applicants is $5.9 billion, or 64 percent of the total funds requested to date. Of the total 626 applications received, 431 were submitted to the FBAs and applicable State regulators for review. The FBAs have completed their reviews of 40 applications. As of May 9, 2011, no applications had completed the other stages of Treasury's review process needed for an investment decision.

At the time of program launch, Treasury released the program terms for only C corporations. The majority of insured depository institutions, bank holding companies, and savings and loan holding companies are C corporations. These institutions were originally given until March 31, 2011, to apply, but this date was recently extended to May 16, 2011. Treasury has not yet established the terms of participation for S corporations, mutual institutions, and CDLFs, as policy changes may be needed regarding either the type of securities that Treasury would purchase from these institutions, or the criteria under which these institutions would be evaluated.

According to Treasury officials, under Internal Revenue Service (IRS) rules, S corporations can have only a single class of stock (common shares). Consequently, these institutions cannot issue preferred stock to Treasury. As a result, Treasury is considering purchasing subordinated debt from these institutions, which the FBAs would likely designate as Tier 2 capital. Treasury officials believe that providing Tier 2 capital would probably result in fewer S corporation participants, as it is unlikely that such institutions would pay the program interest rates for this type of capital.

Additionally, because mutual institutions do not issue stock, Treasury will be unable to receive preferred stock as consideration for an investment in this type of institution. Therefore, Treasury is considering purchasing subordinated debt from these institutions as well.

Treasury must establish alternative means for evaluating the financial viability and repayment ability of CDLFs, which are not regulated or reviewed by the FBAs. Treasury officials stated that they are retaining an outside agent to perform due diligence reviews of CDLF applicants, and developing specific criteria for repayment analyses. In addition to developing the terms for S corporations, mutual institutions, and CDLFs, Treasury —as required under the statute— must also issue regulations to permit the refinancing of CPP and CDCI securities. Treasury has drafted the regulations, and plans to issue them as interim final rules in late spring 2011. Until then, Treasury will be unable to approve applicants attempting to refinance CPP and CDCI investments through SBLF.

At the time of our audit, Treasury had developed, but not finalized all components of the SBLF investment decision process. For example, although Treasury began sending applications to the FBAs in January 2011, it did not reach agreement on the form of consultation to be provided by the FBAs or enter into an MOU with them until March 15, 2011. Representatives from the FBAs told the OIG that they planned to employ the same review process of SBLF applicants as they had for TARP applicants. However, despite expectations of significant similarities between TARP and SBLF processes, it took Treasury several months of negotiations with the FBAs to reach agreement on the type and form of consultation. The parties needed to resolve whether the FBAs would be recommending approval for investment, confirming whether an applicant's CAMELS rating was valid at the time of application, validating the future viability of the applicant, or predicting the probability of loss of the investment. There was also discussion among FBAs regarding the definition of viability and whether viability is a moment-in-time analysis or predictive.

Treasury and the FBAs ultimately agreed that FBAs would advise Treasury only on the financial viability of applicants and their capacity to increase small business lending, and that they would not make investment recommendations as they had for TARP. It was agreed that an applicant would be considered "viable" if it was (1) adequately capitalized; (2) not expected to become undercapitalized; and (3) not expected to be placed into conservatorship or receivership. Further, the FBA's validation of viability of an applicant would reflect only currently available supervisory information and rating assessments at the time the validation was made and would not predict Treasury's loss from making an investment in the institution.

Additionally, policy documents and evaluation guidance for the other steps of the investment decision process were still in draft form as of late March 2011. For example, Treasury had not finalized review checklists and guidance to be used by the Treasury Application Review Team and Application Review Committee. Further, Treasury began working on a conceptual framework for operations in November 2010, but had not formally documented the controls for the various stages of its investment decision process until late March 2011.

Treasury expects that it could take over 120 days for institutions to receive funding after submitting an application. The investment decision process would take 2 to 3 months, and an additional 30 days or more would be needed for the closing and funding processes, including calculation of the baseline level of small business lending and initial dividend rate.

Investment Decision Process

Since November 2010, Treasury officials have been working to define and implement activities that will support its "concept of operations" for SBLF, which was jointly developed with a third-party contractor. This operating model leverages the investment decision process developed for the TARP CPP and CDCI programs and tailors it for the SBLF program. The most significant difference between the TARP and SBLF process is that FBAs will not manage the application process or recommend institutions for investment. Additional information regarding the difference between the TARP and SBLF programs can be found in Appendix 2.

Under the concept of operations shown in Figure 1, all SBLF applications will undergo an 8-step investment evaluation and decision process, except that CPP and CDCI banks will not be considered for approval based on matching funds.

Figure 1: **SBLF Investment Evaluation and Decision Process**

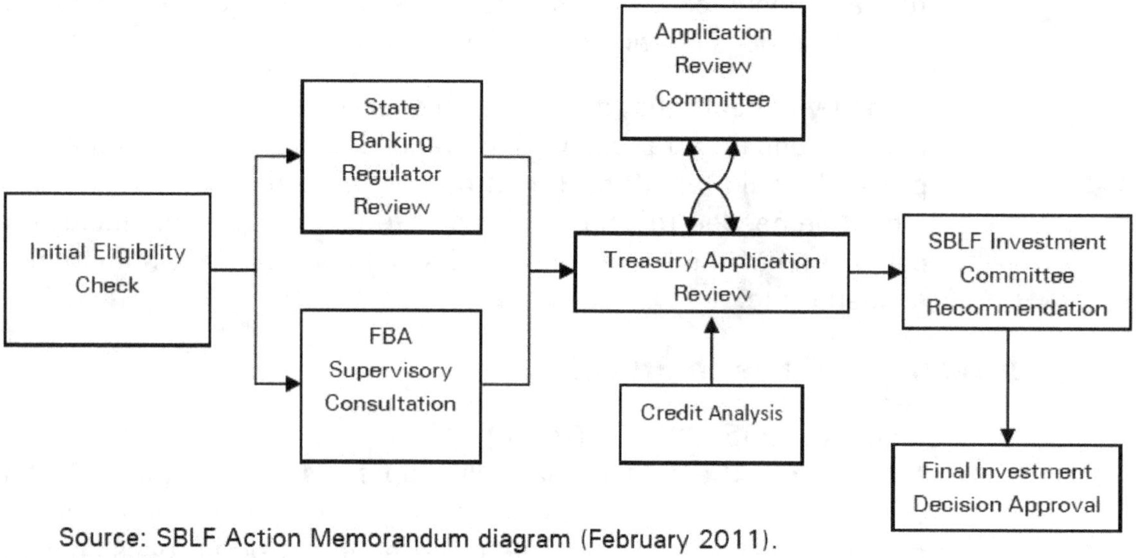

```
                        ┌──────────────┐
                        │ Application  │
                        │   Review     │
                        │  Committee   │
                        └──────┬───────┘
           ┌──────────┐        ↕
           │  State   │        │
       ┌──→│ Banking  │──┐     │
       │   │Regulator │  │     │
       │   │  Review  │  │     │
       │   └──────────┘  │     │
┌──────────┐             ↓  ┌──────────┐   ┌──────────────┐
│ Initial  │            ┌──────────┐   │SBLF Investment│
│Eligibility│           │Treasury  │──→│  Committee   │
│  Check   │            │Application│   │Recommendation│
└──────────┘            │  Review  │   └──────┬───────┘
       │   ┌──────────┐  └──────────┘         │
       │   │   FBA    │  ↑                    ↓
       └──→│Supervisory│─┘  ┌──────────┐  ┌──────────────┐
           │Consultation│    │  Credit  │  │Final Investment│
           └──────────┘    │ Analysis │  │Decision Approval│
                           └──────────┘  └──────────────┘
```

Source: SBLF Action Memorandum diagram (February 2011).

Initial Eligibility Check

The SBLF Investment Team will perform an initial eligibility check based on publically available information to determine whether the applicant meets program eligibility requirements. Specifically, the team will verify that the institution has: (1) less than $10 billion in assets; (2) requested funding totaling no more than 5 percent of its risk-weighted assets if total assets are less than $1 billion, or no more than 3 percent of its risk-weighted assets if total assets exceed $1 billion; and (3) applied at the appropriate ownership level. If the applicant is refinancing its CPP or CDCI position, Treasury will also confirm that the institution has not missed more than one dividend payment and is in compliance with the terms of its TARP CPP or CDCI capital program.

FBA Supervisory Consultation

As required by the Small Business Jobs Act, Treasury will consult with the appropriate FBA[6] for each eligible institution to determine whether the applicant meets the financial requirements for SBLF eligibility. The designated FBA will determine whether the applicant has a CAMELS composite rating of 3 or better, and has not been on the FDIC problem bank list within the last 90 days. The FBA will also validate the

---

[6] In the case of CDLFs, which are not regulated, the SBLF program office would consult with Treasury's Community Development Financial Institutions Fund.

applicant's financial viability based on current confidential supervisory information, which includes examination results, financial ratings, and financial performance ratios. In the event that an applicant is owned by a holding company with multiple subsidiaries, or has significant on- or off-balance sheet activities, the FBA responsible for the bank holding company will also consider the rating and performance ratios at the holding company level and provide a separate consultation to Treasury.

The FBA's validation of viability does not constitute a recommendation that Treasury should invest in the applicant, as Treasury is responsible for ultimately making the investment decision. Instead, the FBAs may inform Treasury on material supervisory issues, including risk management and compliance issues, on-going concerns regarding the financial condition of the institution, the enforcement actions placed on the institution, and any other issues that it believes are not consistent with the receipt of a capital investment. The FBA may also advise Treasury on whether an institution should be required to raise matching capital as a condition of participation in the program. The FBAs may modify their supervisory input at any time before the investment is made. Treasury will not consider an application without a positive validation of viability from the appropriate FBA.

In addition to consultation on the institution's financial viability, FBAs will review the small business lending plan of each applicant from a safety and soundness perspective. The purpose of this review is to assess the applicant's ability to manage the projected increase in small business lending.

State Banking Regulator Review

State banking regulators will also be given the opportunity to review and comment on the financial condition of the applicant; however, their input is not required.

Application Review Committee

The Application Review Committee is a deliberative body made up of current banking supervisors detailed to Treasury. The role of the committee is to ensure that the supervisory consultation process is applied effectively across SBLF investment decisions, and provide recommendations to Treasury on certain SBLF applicants as an additional control point and quality assurance mechanism. The Application Review Committee will review institutions that:

1) Have a composite CAMELS/Rating for Financial Institution (RFI)[7] rating of 3;

2) Have a composite CAMELS/RFI rating of 2 for which the most recent examination is more than 12 months old or for which subsequent quarterly offsite reviews suggest potential deterioration;

3) Have a composite CAMELS/RFI rating of 1 or 2 but have one or more adverse performance ratios;

4) Are required to raise matching capital as a condition of participation as deemed by the appropriate FBA;

5) Do not meet the minimum acceptable probability of repayment in the credit analysis;

6) Receive supervisory input from their State banking regulator that is inconsistent with that of the FBA; or

7) Are otherwise recommended for review by the Treasury Application Review Team (or by the appropriate FBA).

In addition, the Application Review Committee will be asked to review any application that does not receive a positive supervisory consultation. However, the Application Review Committee will not review any application that has been determined to be ineligible to receive capital from the program.

Credit Analysis

Financial agents under contract with Treasury will perform a credit analysis to assess the probability of repayment of the SBLF investment. Institutions must have at least an 80 percent probability of repayment to qualify for the program. A critical part of this analysis will be a forward-looking projection of the institution's cash flows (earnings). In projecting cash flows, the financial agents will review each applicant's asset quality, capital structure, capital adequacy and access to funding, earnings power, and business model. Treasury's financial agents will also consider the institution's forward ratio of Tier 1 common equity to risk-weighted

---

[7] According to the Federal Reserve's *Bank Holding Company Supervision Manual*, RFI ratings are the equivalent of a bank's CAMELS ratings, but are applied at the holding company level.

assets, which Treasury believes to be the most statistically significant factor in predicting bank defaults.[8]

In addition, financial agents will perform targeted topical and industry research on the small-cap bank sector to provide Treasury with industry trends and developments relevant to the credit sector. In these cases, the information provided will not be specific to a given applicant and would not be a direct input to the investment decision process for any one applicant.

Treasury Application Review

The Treasury Application Review Team (will prepare a recommendation memorandum for the SBLF Investment Committee based on a review of (1) the supervisory consultation provided by the FBAs, (2) input from the Application Review Committee, (3) the probability of repayment analysis provided by the financial agents, (4) the opinions of State banking regulators, where applicable, (5) the institution's small business lending plan, and (6) other available non-public inputs, if applicable.

SBLF Investment Committee Recommendation

A 5-member Treasury Investment Committee will consider the Application Review Team's recommendation and the institution's application package and will issue a recommendation to the Secretary, or designee. In making its recommendation, it can also request additional information from any previous step of the application process. The committee will be chaired by the SBLF Program Director and staffed by representatives from the Offices of Financial Institutions, Financial Markets, and Economic Policy.

Final Investment Decision Approval

The Secretary, or designee, will review the Investment Committee's recommendation and make the final investment decision.

---

[8] FRB used this ratio in its 2009 stress test of the 19 largest bank holding companies.

The Program Targets Institutions with Adequate Capital for Lending and Repayment, but Small Business Lending Potential Will Not Be Fully Assessed

Treasury's investment decision process, which closely follows legislative requirements, targets financially viable institutions. Treasury officials believe that this restriction will ensure that banks approved for SBLF funding have the capital needed to repay Treasury's investment and to increase their loans to small businesses. Although the Small Business Jobs Act requires applicants to submit plans outlining goals for increasing small business lending, neither Treasury officials nor the FBAs will evaluate the likelihood of goal achievement.

Capitally-Impaired Banks Are Ineligible for the Program

According to Treasury officials, the SBLF program is designed to target those banks with sufficient capital to repay Treasury's investment and to increase small business lending. Under the terms established by the Small Business Jobs Act, only banks with composite CAMELS ratings of 1, 2, or 3 are eligible for the SBLF program. Composite ratings of 1 or 2 are given to banks with the strongest performance based on capital adequacy, asset quality, management, earnings, liquidity, and sensitivity to market risk. Financial institutions with a composite CAMELS rating of 3 exhibit some degree of supervisory concern in one or more component areas. Only those banks in the three highest CAMELS rating categories that are then determined by the FBAs to be financially viable will be considered for an investment. A determination of financial viability means that the bank is adequately capitalized, and is not expected to become undercapitalized. If supervisory input is received indicating capital inadequacy or other concerns about banks rated 1, 2, or 3, Treasury may approve such banks contingent on receipt of matching capital prior to funding. Treasury officials expect to rarely invoke the matching capital requirement.

Further, CPP and CDCI institutions will not be allowed to raise matching capital to meet qualification requirements. These institutions will have to qualify based on their current capital structure, which includes their remaining TARP funds, and be designated as financially viable by their FBA. For some of the TARP banks, the SBLF investment will simply replace the amount of funds invested under TARP. Therefore, institutions refinancing are not likely to receive much, if any, additional capital with which to make small business loans. According to a Treasury official, most of the TARP banks that have applied for SBLF to date have requested capital investments that are only 10 to 30 percent more than their remaining TARP balances.

We believe the investment decision process established by Treasury to be consistent with legislative eligibility requirements. However, to provide greater transparency into the types of institutions approved for program funding, Treasury should report to Congress monthly aggregate data regarding the capital ratios of approved applicants. While we recognize that Treasury cannot share supervisory information provided by FBAs on program applicants, we believe it can and should include in its monthly reports publicly available information from call reports on the capital ratios of banks at the time they are approved for SBLF funding. By doing so, the Congressional oversight committees can be kept informed of whether the program is reaching intended recipients.

Potential for Growth in Small Business Lending Will Not Be Fully Assessed

As currently designed, the investment decision process does not consider whether applicants will be able to achieve their small business lending goals. As required by legislation, each institution that applies for an SBLF investment must submit a small business lending plan to its respective FBA, or for state-chartered banks, to its State banking regulator. Based on guidance issued by Treasury, the plan must identify the institution's small business lending goals, describe how the applicant's business strategy and operating goals will allow it to address the needs of small businesses in the areas it serves, and outline its outreach plan for attracting borrowers.

Although the small business lending plan is a vital part of an institution's application for the program, neither the FBAs nor Treasury intend to review the likelihood of participants meeting their small business lending goals. The FBAs will review the small business lending plans from only a safety and soundness perspective, assessing whether applicants have the capacity to increase small business lending. However, the FBAs stated that assessing the plan for compliance with SBLF program features should be Treasury's responsibility.

Further, Treasury will review the plans to determine only whether they:

- Include a representation that the applicant will make qualified small business loans in an amount that is equal to or greater than Treasury's SBLF investment.

- Address the needs of small businesses in areas it serves (and describe those needs and the mechanisms it will use to address them).

- Provide the appropriate linguistic and cultural outreach to attract borrowers (and describe one or more mechanisms for such outreach).

Treasury officials do not believe that the reasonableness of an institution's small business lending plan should be a deciding factor for approval as the Small Business Jobs Act does not require participants to increase their small business lending. Further, officials believe that the legislation incents banks to increase small business lending through dividend reductions (or a dividend increase in the event an institution fails to increase lending) to drive the small business lending gains the program sets to achieve.

Because the Small Business Jobs Act provides that Treasury may consult with SBA in administration of the SBLF program, we met with SBA officials to determine how SBA could help Treasury in the investment decision process. We learned that SBA may conduct market research that could help Treasury determine the demand for small business loans in various geographic areas. SBA also has data identifying the volume of the small business lending of various SBA lenders that may be applying to the SBLF program. SBA could help institutions develop outreach plans and business strategies to target and attract small businesses in the areas they serve, as well as provide other types of technical assistance. SBA officials indicated they welcomed consultation with Treasury's SBLF staff as it would provide an opportunity for them to work together to maximize SBLF program outcomes.

Although SBLF participants are not required to increase lending to small businesses, stimulating such lending was clearly the intent of Congress in creating the SBLF program. Therefore, we believe it would be prudent for Treasury to ensure it is investing in banks with the greatest potential for increasing small business lending. Senior Treasury officials indicated that they have been communicating with SBA and are interested in having the SBLF program office explore ways to leverage SBA's data and experience to achieve program outcomes. Further, they acknowledged that their initial focus was on the financial viability and capacity of applicants to responsibly manage growth in small business lending, and are now planning additional steps to ensure that applicants have credible and specific small business lending plans.

SBA Lending History Will Not Be Considered

Treasury officials expect that some lenders applying to the SBLF program may have participated in loan guarantee programs administered by SBA. SBA officials stated that through its oversight and portfolio analysis functions, SBA collects information that could inform Treasury of institutions that are not in compliance with SBA's lending requirements. Such noncompliance would include institutions making loans to businesses that do not qualify as small, are not using loan proceeds as agreed to, and are not making the required equity injection, among other things. Consequently, such information could help alert Treasury to institutions with a history of noncompliance or over-reporting their small business lending.

Despite the availability of such information and indications from Treasury that its Application Review Team may consider other non-public inputs, Treasury has not incorporated steps into the investment decision process to identify current SBA lenders or consulted with SBA to obtain information on the compliance of those lenders with Federal SBA lending requirements.

Other Opportunities for Improvements

Supervisory Consultation Memo Does Not Require Thorough Disclosure

The supervisory consultation memo focuses primarily on performance ratios and CAMELS ratings. The memo allows the FBAs to provide discussion of material supervisory issues in the form of supporting comments in an optional narrative. This allows the FBAs to have significant discretion on the type of information to provide to Treasury. This level of information may have been sufficient under the process established for TARP because the FBAs were responsible for recommending institutions for funding, and thus were stakeholders in the TARP decisions. However, under SBLF, FBAs will not be stakeholders and will not be recommending investments. Rather, Treasury will be making the investment decision; and therefore, will need more robust information with which to make a decision. For this reason, we believe that Treasury should explicitly request more robust information about material supervisory issues for each institution, such as the institution's compliance history, enforcement actions taken against it, and matters requiring attention identified by regulators so that Treasury can make a more informed investment decision.

Criteria for Determining Whether Matching Funds Will Be Required Has Not Been Defined

Treasury officials have not provided guidance as to the circumstances that will warrant a matching capital requirement, but believe that the requirement will rarely be imposed under SBLF as it was rarely applied under the TARP CDCI program. They stated that undercapitalization is most likely an indicator of other problems impacting the institution's financial viability that would prevent an applicant from being approved. Further, Treasury has not issued prescriptive guidance to the FBAs to use in making such determinations because it believes that matching capital will not necessarily improve the supervisory review of the FBAs, and the Application Review Committee will address whether matching capital requirements have been consistently applied.

We believe that the Application Review Committee review will be an effective way to identify inconsistency in decisions involving matching capital as Treasury will ultimately make the decision. However, without guidance from Treasury, FBAs may not identify all of the institutions that should be considered for the matching requirement.

Although the FBAs and Treasury's Application Review Committee, Application Review Team, and Investment Committee can all impose the matching capital requirement, we believe that defined criteria for the FBAs would add clarity to an important aspect of the legislation and the investment decision process.

The Non-Cumulative Treatment of Dividends May Result in Institutions Not Fully Paying Dividends Owed on Treasury's Investment

Under the terms set by legislation, dividend payments are non-cumulative, meaning that institutions are under no obligation to make dividend payments as scheduled or to pay off previously missed payments before exiting the program. This dividend treatment differs from the TARP programs, in which many dividend payments were cumulative. This change in dividend treatment was driven by changes in capital requirements mandated by the Collins Amendment to the Dodd-Frank Act.[9]

The amendment equalizes the consolidated capital requirements for Tier 1 capital of bank holding companies by requiring that, at a minimum, regulators apply the same capital and risk standards for FDIC-insured banks to bank holding companies. Under TARP, the FRB and FDIC treated capital differently at the holding company and depository institution levels. The FRB treated cumulative securities issued by holding companies as Tier 1 capital, while FDIC treated non-cumulative securities issued by depository institutions as Tier 1 capital. In order to comply with the Dodd-Frank Act requirement that securities purchased from holding companies receive the same capital treatment as those purchased from depository institutions, Treasury made the dividends under SBLF non-cumulative.

Additionally, given that Tier 1 capital must be perpetual and cannot have a mandatory redemption date, the 10-year repayment period[10] in the Small Business Jobs Act cannot be enforced. However, to encourage repayment, Treasury has placed the following additional requirements and restrictions on participants who miss dividend payments:

- The participant's CEO and CFO must provide written notice regarding the rationale of the board of directors (BOD) for not declaring a dividend.

- No repurchases may be affected and no dividends may be declared on any securities for the applicable quarter and the following three quarters.

- After four missed payments (consecutive or not), the issuer's BOD must certify in writing that the issuer used best efforts to declare and pay dividends appropriately.

- After five missed payments (consecutive or not), Treasury may appoint a representative to serve as an observer on the issuer's BOD.

---

[9] Section 171 of Public Law 111-203.
[10] The repayment deadline can be extended or waived if it would adversely affect the capital treatment of the stock or financial instrument.

- After six missed payments (consecutive or not), Treasury may elect two directors to the issuer's BOD if the liquidation preference is $25 million or more.

Treasury believes that both the considerable reputational risk of non-payment and the program incentives for payment will help mitigate the use of a non-cumulative security in the SBLF program. We agree that Treasury's equity investment is consistent with the legislation and that it has reasonably structured the program to incentivize payment of dividends.

However, because dividends are non-cumulative under the Small Business Jobs Act, Treasury has no recourse to require dividend payments as a condition for exiting the SBLF program unless Congress were to amend the Small Business Jobs Act to clarify whether all dividends must be repaid upon exiting the program and/or seek a waiver from the Collins Amendment to the Dodd-Frank Act. We note that Section 171(b)(5) of the Dodd-Frank Act fully exempted securities issued to the Federal government before the end of the TARP investment period on October 4, 2010, from the capital treatment provisions added by the Collins Amendment. This exemption allowed Treasury to receive cumulative securities under TARP.

Recommendations

Based on our audit of the SBLF investment decision process, we recommend that Treasury:

1) Report monthly to Congress aggregate data on the capital ratios of institutions at the time they are approved for SBLF funding, which is publicly available in call reports.

    Management Response

    Treasury officials agreed with this recommendation and stated they will include aggregate data on publicly-available regulatory capital ratios in the monthly transaction reports published for SBLF.

    OIG Comments

    Management's proposed actions are responsive to the OIG's recommendation.

2) Consult with SBA in making investment decisions to determine the achievability of small business lending goals and identify compliance associated with applicants who are or were SBA lenders.

Management Response

Treasury officials agreed with the OIG that information regarding the performance record of current or former SBA lenders applying for SBLF funding could serve as a useful input to SBLF investment decisions. Following consultation with the OIG, Treasury initiated discussions with SBA in early March to obtain access to this information. While these discussions are ongoing, Treasury officials indicated they would welcome the opportunity to incorporate such data into SBLF investment decisions.

Treasury officials also stated they are implementing a comprehensive review process for small business lending plans to ensure that SBLF applicants submit responsive plans that establish specific lending goals. In this context, officials stated they will continue to explore ways in which the SBA could support Treasury's assessment of these plans. They reported that to date, the applicability of SBA market research with respect to SBLF has been limited because:

1. SBLF is a new initiative that is designed to foster increased credit availability by providing banks with the financial capacity and incentives to increase small business lending in local markets. These forward-looking effects may not be fully incorporated in retrospective analyses of market demand.

2. The conventional bank lending market addressed by SBLF has not been correlated with SBA lending in recent years due, in part, to the economic downturn and temporary enhancements to SBA programs (e.g., increased guarantee levels and fee waivers). Consequently, measures of an institution's SBA lending may not be indicative of potential lending increases under SBLF.

3. SBA lending programs and associated reports employ materially different definitions of "small business lending" and underwriting standards than those that are statutorily mandated for SBLF. These differences yield the potential for

significant inconsistencies in comparisons of SBA and SBLF lending patterns.

Treasury appreciates this recommendation and will continue to assess additional ways in which SBA resources could supplement Treasury's evaluation of applicants' small business lending goals.

OIG Comments

Management's proposed actions are responsive to the OIG's recommendation.

3) Identify opportunities where SBA can provide technical assistance to institutions to help increase small business lending and maximize program outcomes.

Management Response

Treasury officials agreed with this recommendation. They stated that since the passage of the Small Business Jobs Act, Treasury and SBA officials have worked in tandem to coordinate the agencies' implementation of the Act, including briefings regarding SBLF program terms and status for SBA leadership and field office staff.

As institutions begin to receive SBLF funding, Treasury officials anticipate there will be additional opportunities to further deepen these relationships and foster collaboration among SBA, Treasury, and SBLF participants to maximize the program's results.

OIG Comments

Management's proposed actions are responsive to the OIG's recommendation.

4) Modify the supervisory consultation form to require that FBAs provide more robust information on applicants beyond performance ratios and CAMELS ratings, such as history of compliance, enforcement actions, and matters requiring attention.

Management Response

Treasury officials indicated that they share the OIG's interest in ensuring that comprehensive supervisory input is made available for each applicant, and they have consulted the FBAs regarding this recommendation.

They stated that the supervisory consultation memorandum requires the FBAs to complete a written narrative for each applicant with respect to material supervisory issues, including the on-going financial condition of the institution and enforcement actions, if any.

According to Treasury officials, the FBAs have indicated to Treasury that the types of information cited in this recommendation constitute material supervisory issues that would be subject to inclusion in the supervisory consultation memorandum. In addition, the FBAs have told Treasury officials that they complete multiple internal reviews of each consultation prior to submission. Treasury officials stated that they also conduct a review of each consultation upon receipt to further validate the information provided.

OIG Comments

Although management officials did not agree to modify the supervisory consultation form to specify the types of information that must be in the narrative, the OIG considers Treasury's comments to be responsive. However, the OIG will follow-up to ensure that the FBAs are reporting all material supervisory issues on the supervisory consultative memorandum.

5) Establish a process that confirms with the FBAs that there has been no change in the safety and soundness or viability of the applicant, and that there have been no new supervisory concerns identified prior to disbursement of funds for all applicants.

Management Response

Treasury officials generally agreed with this recommendation, indicating that they have implemented such a procedure. According to Treasury officials, the FBAs notify Treasury on an ongoing basis as they are made aware of material information regarding an applicant that becomes available following submission of the supervisory consultation memorandum. In addition, Treasury also monitors each applicant's public filings to assess any changes in its financial condition.

OIG Comments

The OIG does not believe that monitoring public filings is an effective way to identify material supervisory issues that may occur subsequent to the supervisory consultation as such issues may not be made public. Also, relying on the FBAs to notify Treasury of changes in material information affecting applicant eligibility may not be the most effective means of obtaining assurance that approved applicants remain eligible. We believe that Treasury should exercise greater due diligence by contacting the FBAs prior to funding to confirm there has been no change in the financial viability of applicants as FBAs may forget to notify Treasury of any changes and will not have knowledge of the timing of Treasury's funding decision.

6) Develop matching capital guidance for the FBAs that detail Treasury's expectations of the FBAs with both general principles and specific parameters. Include sample scenarios that can demonstrate the types of factors that should warrant consideration of matching funds – e.g., ranges of performance ratios, individual CAMELS component ratings, etc.

Management Response

Treasury officials indicated that they maintain an ongoing dialogue with the FBAs regarding the supervisory consultation process for SBLF, including the application of the matching capital provision.

Based on these discussions, Treasury officials indicated their understanding is that there are only limited circumstances – often unique to a specific institution – in which the addition of matching capital alone would alter an FBA's viability assessment. This is because weakness in an institution's regulatory capital position is most frequently a consequence, and not a cause, of deficient performance with respect to other supervisory elements such as management, asset quality, and earnings.

Examples of situations Treasury has reviewed with the FBAs for which matching capital may be appropriate include certain institutions that have experienced: (1) significant losses in their securities portfolio, the source of which would not otherwise prompt concerns regarding investment or asset-liability management practices, (2) a temporary impairment arising from a natural disaster or similar finite event, and (3) historical losses that have reduced capital levels, even as the institution has resolved legacy asset quality challenges and returned to profitability.

In line with this recommendation, Treasury officials agreed to document these scenarios in written guidance. Because many such situations are institution-specific in nature, Treasury officials stated they have also established the policy that the Application Review Committee – a team of experienced banking supervisors detailed to Treasury – will review any application for which an FBA suggests matching capital or does not provide a positive validation of viability. The purpose of these reviews is to ensure that the supervisory consultation process is effectively applied across all applications, including those for which matching capital may be relevant

OIG Comments

Management's proposed actions are responsive to the OIG's recommendation.

Matter for Congressional Consideration

We are suggesting that Congress consider whether an amendment to the Small Business Jobs Act and/or waiver from the Collins Amendment to the Dodd-Frank Act is needed to make the repayment of dividends a requirement for exiting the program.

* * * * *

We appreciate the courtesies and cooperation provided to our staff during the audit. If you wish to discuss the report, you may contact me at (202) 927-0384.

Debra Ritt
Special Deputy Inspector General for
Office of Small Business Lending Fund Program Oversight

Appendix 1
Objectives, Scope, and Methodology

We conducted this audit of the Small Business Lending Fund (SBLF) in response to our mandate under section 4107 of the Small Business Jobs Act of 2010.[11] This section provides that the Office of SBLF Program Oversight is responsible for audit and investigations related to the SBLF program and must report at least twice a year to the Secretary of the Treasury and Congress on the results of oversight activities, including recommended program improvements.

We initiated an audit of the investment decision process for SBLF on January 20, 2011, pursuant to Section 4107 of the Small Business Jobs Act. Our objectives were to determine whether the review process established by Treasury ensures that (1) eligible institutions in need of capital or with the most potential for small business lending are approved, and (2) investments are made in institutions with good track records of performance and compliance with Federal lending requirements.

At the time of the audit, Treasury had established an investment decision framework, but major elements of the framework had not been finalized. Therefore, our audit focused largely on the first two stages of the process that were most defined—the initial eligibility check and Federal Banking Agency (FBA)[12] consultation, which were finalized in March 2011. We reviewed pre-decisional policies and procedures for other stages of the investment decision process, but sufficient information was not available to perform a detailed analysis.

To accomplish our objectives, we reviewed the draft concept of operations for the decision process, procedural guidance, memoranda of understanding (MOUs) between Treasury and the FBAs, consultative decision templates to be used by the FBAs and evaluation checklists established by Treasury. We also reviewed the program application form, outreach guidance to eligible institutions, and program terms. Further, at our request, SBLF responded in writing to OIG questions, providing explanations of initial program focus and critical path activities.

We interviewed SBLF program staff, contractor personnel, and officials from each of the FBAs. The interviews with the FBAs involved

---

[11] The Small Business Jobs Act of 2010, Public Law 111-240, was signed into law on September 27, 2010.
[12] The FBAs are the Office of the Comptroller of the Currency, the Office of Thrift Supervision, the Federal Deposit Insurance Corporation (FDIC), and the Federal Reserve Board (FRB).

Appendix 1
Objectives, Scope, and Methodology

discussions about their processes for determining the financial viability of institutions applying for capital under SBLF. In addition, we met with officials from the Small Business Administration (SBA) to discuss potential lender performance and compliance data as well as small business lending market statistics that could be shared with Treasury officials.

We conducted our fieldwork from January through March 2011 and prepared this report in accordance with Government Auditing Standards. Those standards require that we plan and perform the audit to obtain sufficient, appropriate evidence to provide a reasonable basis for our findings and conclusions based on our audit objectives. We believe that the evidence obtained provides a reasonable basis for our findings and conclusions based on our audit objectives.

Appendix 2
Comparison of TARP – CPP/CDCI and SBLF

	TARP - CPP/CDCI	**SBLF**
Overall Goal	To stabilize and strengthen the U.S. financial system by increasing the capital base of viable institutions, enabling them to lend to consumers and businesses	To address the ongoing effects of the financial crisis on small businesses by providing temporary authority to the Secretary of the Treasury to make capital investments in eligible institutions in order to increase the availability of credit for small businesses
Authorization	$700 billion	$30 billion
Structure	An institution's participation in the Troubled Asset Relief Program (TARP) could fall under multiple areas: 1) Capital Purchase Program (CPP) 2) Term Asset-Backed Securities Loan Facility (TALF) 3) Commercial Paper Funding Facility (CPFF) 4) Debt Guarantee and Temporary Liquidity Guarantee Program (TLGP) 5) Troubled Asset Insurance Finance Fund (TAIFF) 6) Community Development Credit Initiative (CDCI)	An institution's participation in the Small Business Lending Fund (SBLF) would only link the entity to SBLF
Participation	No exclusions based on assets No exclusions based on CAMELS ratings No exclusions based on the Problem Bank List	Issuer must have total consolidated assets equal to or less than $10 billion as of the end of calendar year 2009 Congress allows CPP/CDCI institutions to refinance into the SBLF Issuer must redeem all outstanding CPP or CDCI preferred stock on or prior to the Treasury investment date All CAMELS 4 and 5 rated banks are excluded Banks that are or have been on the FDIC Problem Bank List within the last 90 days are excluded

Appendix 2
Comparison of TARP – CPP/CDCI and SBLF

	Maximum investment under CPP – 3 percent of risk-weighted assets (RWA)[13] capped at $25 billion Maximum investment for issuers under CDCI – 5 percent of RWA	Maximum investment for issuers with $1 billion or less in total assets or that are Community Development Loan Funds (CDLF) – 5 percent of RWA Maximum investment for issuers with $1 billion to $10 billion in total assets or that are required to seek matching private capital investment – 3 percent of RWA

Dividends	Dividends are cumulative or non-cumulative
	
	5 percent annually until the fifth year (CPP)
	
	2 percent annually until the eighth year (CDCI)
	
	Following initial 5-year period, rate will be 9 percent (CPP)
	
	Following initial 8-year period, rate will be 9 percent (CDCI)
		Dividends are non-cumulative
		
		Initial rate of 5 percent annually, adjusted quarterly for approximately the first 2 years (9 calendar quarters) based on small business lending. When lending increases:
		   1) by less than 2.5 percent, the adjusted rate will be 5 percent
		
		   2) by at least 2.5 percent but less than 5 percent, the adjusted rate will be 4 percent
		   3) by at least 5 percent but less than 7.5 percent, the adjusted rate will be 3 percent
		   4) by at least 7.5 percent but less than 10 percent, the adjusted rate will be 2 percent
		   5) by 10 percent or greater, the adjusted rate will be 1 percent
		
		Following initial 2-year (10 calendar quarters) period, if small business lending has remained the same or decreased, the adjusted rate will be 7 percent
		
		Following initial 4.5-year period, the adjusted rate will be 9 percent
		
		CDLF -- rate will be 2 percent annually for the first 8 years, then 9 percent

Repayment	No restrictions until 5 missed payments[14]	**For any missed payment**, restrictions will apply including:
		   1) the issuer's CEO and CFO must provide written notice regarding the rationale of the board of directors (BOD) for not declaring dividends
		   2) prohibiting dividends for the applicable quarter and the following 3 quarters

---

[13] The risk-weighted asset amount is determined as of the call report immediately preceding the date of application, less the amount of any CDCI investment and any CPP investment.
[14] A dividend payment is considered "missed" after 60 days.

Appendix 2
Comparison of TARP – CPP/CDCI and SBLF

		After 4 missed payments (consecutive or not), the issuer's BOD must certify in writing that the issuer used best efforts to declare and pay dividends appropriately
	After 5 missed payments (consecutive or not), Treasury may appoint representatives to serve as an observers of the issuer's BOD	After 5 missed payments (consecutive or not), Treasury may appoint a representative to serve as an observer of the issuer's BOD
	After 6 missed payments (consecutive or not), Treasury may elect 2 directors to the issuer's BOD	After 6 missed payments (consecutive or not), if the liquidation preference is $25 million or more, Treasury may elect 2 directors to the issuer's BOD
		For CPP participants[15], if at the beginning of the tenth full quarter after investment date, small business lending has not increased, issuer must pay a lending incentive fee of 2 percent annually of the aggregate liquidation preference
		Lending incentive fee will end 4.5years after the investment date
	To repay all or part of the investment, issuer must pay a minimum of 25 percent of the issue price of the preferred stock	To repay any part of the investment, issuer must pay a minimum of 25 percent of the number of originally issued shares or 100 percent of the then-outstanding shares, if less than 25 percent of the originally issued shares
Restrictions & Requirements[16]	General usage requirement on the capital invested including the expansion of the flow of capital	Capital investment must be used to increase small business lending or suffer increased dividend rate
		May not invest in a CPP participant that has missed more than 1 dividend payment under CPP
		Require the issuer to provide linguistically and culturally appropriate outreach and advertising
		Applicable Federal Banking Agency (FBA) (or the like) must issue guidance on underwriting standards to be used for loans made using SBLF funds within 60 days

---

[15] CPP participant refers to an issuer that participated in CPP and did not redeem, or apply to redeem, the CPP investment on or before December 16, 2010.
[16] All reporting requirements of the Program, the Inspector General of the Department of the Treasury and the Government Accountability Office are not listed in this table.

Appendix 2
Comparison of TARP – CPP/CDCI and SBLF

		Treasury may take actions the Secretary deems necessary to carry out authority given under the legislation
	Consider factors which include:	Consider factors which include:
	1) providing financial assistance to financial institutions, including those serving low- and moderate-income or underserved areas,	1) providing funding to minority-owned eligible institutions and other institutions that serve minority-, veteran-, and women-owned as well as low- and moderate-income, underserved, or rural areas,
	2) providing stability and preventing disruption of financial markets,	2) increasing the opportunity for small business development in areas with high unemployment,
	3) the need to keep families in their homes, and	3) providing funding to eligible institutions that serve communities that have suffered negative economic effects due to the 2010 offshore drilling unit failure along the coast of the Gulf of Mexico, and
	4) minimizing cost to taxpayers	4) minimizing cost to taxpayers
	Prior to January 2009, there were no requirements for recipients to report on their use of TARP funds	Treasury must provide a written report to Congress detailing how participants have used the funds received under the SBLF, within 7 days after the end of each quarter
		Quarterly reporting requirement for recipients and recalculation of dividend
Application Review Process	No required state input	Requires consultation with appropriate FBA (or the Community Development Financial Institution (CDFI) Fund for non-depository CDFIs) and consideration of state input (if provided)
	Advisory board members (CPP Council) are FBA representatives	Application Review Committee members are Treasury representatives
	Applications start with FBAs	Applications start with Treasury
	FBAs provide Treasury with recommendation for investment	FBAs do not provide Treasury with recommendation for investment
	All analysis performed by FBAs	Credit analysis performed under Treasury
	FBA or CPP Council recommendation goes to Investment Committee	Application Review Team receives supervisory input and credit analysis before sending to the Investment Committee
		Issuer is required to submit a small business lending plan to the FBA or applicable state regulator
Miscellaneous	Programs under TARP did not require a new organization	Requires new program formation and establishment of new organization

Appendix 2
Comparison of TARP – CPP/CDCI and SBLF

	SBLF is established as separate and distinct from TARP -- Recipient of SBLF capital investment is not as a result also considered to be a recipient of TARP
	Assurance that if a subsequent change in law modifies the terms of the investment under the Program in a manner that materially adversely affects the issuer, the issuer, after consultation with the applicable FBA, may repay the investment without impediment
Restrictions on executive compensation	No restrictions on executive compensation
No formal outreach performed -- bailout program highly publicized	Outreach to banks necessary -- Call center and outreach materials needed
Allows for Treasury to purchase warrants	No allowance for Treasury to purchase warrants

Appendix 3
Management's Response

DEPARTMENT OF THE TREASURY
WASHINGTON, D.C. 20220

May 12, 2011

Debra Ritt
Special Deputy Inspector General for
Small Business Lending Fund Oversight
U.S. Department of the Treasury
1500 Pennsylvania Avenue, NW
Washington, DC 20220

Dear Ms. Ritt:

Thank you for the opportunity to review and comment on your draft report regarding the investment decision process for the Small Business Lending Fund (SBLF).

We appreciate your staff's collaborative approach in evaluating policies and procedures related to the investment decision process while these remained under development. The insights and guidance offered by your staff over the course of this audit have helped strengthen this process in advance of any investment of taxpayer funds.

Your draft report recognizes that Treasury's investment decision process closely follows the legislative requirements of the Small Business Jobs Act of 2010. In implementing this process, Treasury has sought to establish policies that maximize the likelihood that institutions will use SBLF funding to increase their lending to small businesses while protecting the taxpayer's investment.

Treasury has given careful consideration to each of the six recommendations presented in this report. Through discussions with your staff, we have already incorporated several of these recommendations into our existing processes. As three of the report's recommendations relate to Treasury's consultation with the federal banking agencies, we have shared these recommendations with those agencies as well.

The enclosed management response provides a more comprehensive description of the steps Treasury is taking with respect to the report's recommendations.

In closing, I would like to reiterate my appreciation of the constructive relationship we have developed with you and your team. We look forward to continuing to work together as we implement this important new initiative.

Sincerely,

Don Graves, Jr.
Deputy Assistant Secretary for Small Business,
Community Development, and Affordable
Housing Policy

Appendix 4
Report Distribution

Department of the Treasury
    Deputy Secretary
    Office of Strategic Planning and Performance Management
    Office of Accounting and Internal Control

Office of the Comptroller of the Currency
    Acting Comptroller of the Currency
    Liaison Officer

Office of Management and Budget
    OIG Budget Examiner

Federal Deposit Insurance Corporation
    Chairman
    Inspector General

Federal Reserve Board
    Chairman
    Inspector General

United States Senate
    Chairman and Ranking Member
    Committee on Small Business and Entrepreneurship

    Chairman and Ranking Member
    Committee on Finance

United States House of Representatives
    Chairman and Ranking Member
    Committee on Small Business

    Chairman and Ranking Member
    Committee on Financial Services

Government Accountability Office
    Comptroller General of the United States

www.ingramcontent.com/pod-product-compliance
Lightning Source LLC
Chambersburg PA
CBHW081806170526
45167CB00008B/3342